MW01147441

A Pocket Guide to

The Meaning of Life

A Pocket Guide to

The Meaning of Life

Peter Kreeft

Our Sunday Visitor Publishing Division
Our Sunday Visitor, Inc.
Huntington, Indiana 46750

Copyright © 2007 by Our Sunday Visitor Publishing Division, Our Sunday Visitor, Inc. Published 2007

12 11 10 09 08 07   1 2 3 4 5 6 7 8 9

Our Sunday Visitor Publishing Division
Our Sunday Visitor, Inc.
200 Noll Plaza
Huntington, IN 46750

ISBN: 978-1-59276-300-9 (Inventory No. T392)
LCCN: 2006939579

Cover design by Tyler Ottinger
Cover art: Detail of "The Creation of Adam," by Michelangelo, from Planet Art
Interior design by Sherri L. Hoffman

PRINTED IN THE UNITED STATES OF AMERICA

For Mom and Dad,
my first teachers

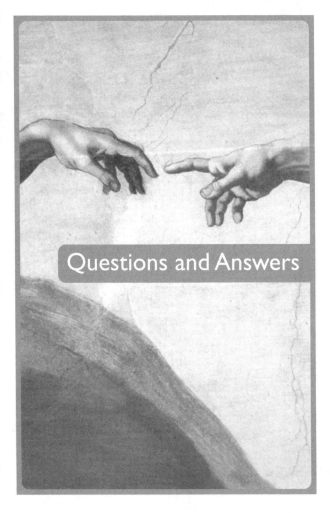

Questions and Answers

1. What must I know to know the meaning of life?

You must know your origin, your nature, and your destiny. Where did you come from, what are you, and where are you going?

2. What is my origin?

In God is the secret of your origin. God is your creator.

3. What is my identity?

In God is the secret of your identity. God is your Father. You are His image.

4. What is my destiny?

In God is the secret of your destiny. God is your Home.

5. Why did God create me?

Out of love. You were loved into existence. You are God's planned and wanted child.

6. What does God want from me?

He wants what any lover wants: the free gift of your love to Him, to match His to you.

7. Is God selfish, to want my love?

No. God wants your love, not because He needs to get it, but because you need to give it.

8. Does God need anything from me?

No. God is perfect, and needs nothing. The motive for His love is pure generosity, not need. But though He needs nothing from you, He wants everything, for He is Infinite Love.

9. What do I need most?

To know God.

A woman named Martha received [Jesus] into her house. And she had a sister called Mary, who sat at the Lord's feet and listened to his teaching. But Martha was distracted with much serving; and she went to him and said, "Lord, do you not care that my sister has left me to serve alone? Tell her then to help me." But the Lord answered her, "Martha, Martha, you are anxious and troubled about many things; one thing is needful. Mary has chosen the good portion, which shall not be taken away from her." (Luke 10:38-42)

10. Isn't this a philosophy for monks and mystics rather than ordinary Christians?

No, because a Christian, at the very least, is one who believes that Christ has given us the very best answer to life's most important question: What is life to the fullest? What is the meaning of life?

Jesus' answer:

"This is eternal life, that they know you the only true God, and Jesus Christ whom you have sent." (John 17:3)

11. What else do I need besides the need to know God?

You need only one thing besides knowing God: you need to know that you need nothing more.

12. Why do I need nothing more?

Because God is not just one good thing among others, but the source of all good, the giver of every good and perfect gift (James 1:17).

One who has God, has everything; and one who has everything except God, has nothing; and one who has God plus everything else has no more than one who has God alone. (St. Augustine)

13. Why doesn't the addition of anything else to God make my life fuller?

Because "this is eternal life [life to the fullest], that they know you the only true God, and Jesus Christ whom you have sent" (John 17:3).

14. If "knowing God" is the meaning of my life, what sort of knowledge is this?

It is personal knowledge — that is, the knowledge *of* a person, not just knowledge *about* him.

15. How can I know God?

Through Jesus Christ.

"He who has seen me has seen the Father." (John 14:9)

16. How can I know Jesus Christ?

Through the Church He founded to teach in His name. "He who hears you hears me" (Luke 10:16). This is, in fact, how you did hear about Him: you were told by disciples, His Church, down through the ages, and by the book they wrote and certified — the New Testament.

17. What does the Church offer me as the way to know God?

Faith, hope, and love.

18. What is faith?

Faith is believing in God, and therefore believing what God has told us. Faith is our yes to God and to His revelation.

19. How has God revealed Himself?

In at least seven ways:

1. In nature, His creation, as an artist is revealed in his art.

2. In human nature, especially in conscience, His inner prophet in your soul.

3. In every truth we discover, every good we do, and every beauty we create.

In addition to this natural revelation, God has also acted supernaturally:

4. In history, by choosing a people (the Jews) to be His collective prophet to the world, making a covenant with them, giving them

His law and His prophets, performing miracles for them (such as the Exodus), and inspiring their sacred Scriptures, which Christians call the "Old Testament."

5. Most completely of all, in sending His own divine Son, Jesus Christ.

6. Through the Church Christ established "upon the foundation of the apostles" (Ephesians 2:20).

7. In the book the apostles authored and the Church authorized, the New Testament.

20. Why can we trust all God's revelations?

Because God can neither deceive nor be deceived. God is Truth.

21. What is hope?

Hope is believing God's promises. Hope is faith directed to the future. Like faith, hope is a response to God's revelation, not a feeling we work up in ourselves. It is like an investment in God. Its opposite is despair, which is giving up on God.

22. How best of all can I know God?

By love.

"You shall love the Lord your God with all your heart, and with all your soul, and with all your mind. This is the great and first commandment." (Matthew 22:37-38)

23. Why is loving God the best way to know God?

For the same reason love is the best way to know a human person. Love (charity) is itself a kind of knowledge, the deepest kind of knowledge of a person.

24. How can love be knowledge? Isn't love blind?

Love is not blind, for "God is love" (1 John 4:8), and God is not blind. Feelings can be blind, but the essence of love is not a feeling.

25. What is the essence of love?

Love is a free gift of one's self to another. Love is a choice, not a feeling. It comes from you, not to you. You do it with your heart, your center, not only with your emotions. That is why "in the evening of our lives, we will be judged on our love" (St. John of the Cross). For God judges justly, and it is not just to judge people on their feelings, which are not in their power, but on their free choices, which are.

26. How can I love God?

There is no technique for love. You "just do it." You "just say yes."

27. What will I do if I love God?

God's answer to that question is: If you love God, you will love your neighbor.

"Truly, I say to you, as you did it to one of the least of these my brethren, you did it to me." (Matthew 25:40; also see Matthew 25:31-46)

28. Who is my neighbor?

Whoever needs you is your neighbor. When Jesus was asked this question, He told the parable of the Good Samaritan (Luke 10:25-37).

29. Am I to love all mankind?

"Mankind" is an abstraction. Your neighbor is concretely real. Christ did not command us to love "mankind" but to love our neighbors, all our neighbors, one at a time.

30. Can I love my neighbor even when I do not feel any love for him?

Yes, just as you love yourself even when you do not feel self-love or self-esteem: you never stop seeking your own true happiness. Christ commands us to do the same to our neighbor.

"You shall love your neighbor as your-self." (Matthew 22:39)

31. How do I love my neighbor?

As with loving God, you "just do it." You freely choose. There is no technique. But though love has no cause, it has effects. Love (charity) serves. Love works.

32. Does it matter *what* I believe, hope, and love?

It matters enormously. To believe what is not true, or to hope for and love what is not good, is bound to harm you (and all those you affect, all those you love), both in this life and in the next.

33. How does the Church summarize what a Catholic Christian believes?

In the Apostles' Creed:

I believe in God,
    the Father almighty,
    creator of heaven and earth.

I believe in Jesus Christ,
    his only Son, our Lord.

He was conceived by the
    power of the Holy Spirit
    and born of the Virgin Mary.

He suffered under Pontius Pilate,
    was crucified, died, and was
        buried.
    He descended into hell.

On the third day he rose again.

He ascended into heaven,
and is seated at the right
hand of the Father.
He will come again to judge
the living and the dead.

I believe in the Holy Spirit,
the holy catholic Church,
the communion of saints,
the forgiveness of sins,
the resurrection of the body,
and the life everlasting. Amen.

34. How does the Church summarize what a Catholic Christian hopes?

In the Lord's Prayer:

Our Father who art in heaven, hallowed be thy name. Thy kingdom come. Thy will be done on earth, as it is in heaven. Give us this day our daily bread, and forgive us our trespasses, as we forgive those who trespass against us, and lead us not into temptation, but deliver us from evil.

35. How does the Church summarize how a Catholic Christian loves?

In the Ten Commandments:

1. I am the LORD your God: you shall not have strange gods before me.
2. You shall not take the name of the LORD your God in vain.
3. Remember to keep holy the LORD'S Day.
4. Honor your father and your mother.
5. You shall not kill.
6. You shall not commit adultery.
7. You shall not steal.
8. You shall not bear false witness against your neighbor.
9. You shall not covet your neighbor's wife.
10. You shall not covet your neighbor's goods.

36. Where did the Apostles' Creed come from?

It is a summary of the teaching of Christ to His apostles, and it was composed by the successors they ordained. *Their* successors still exist today; they are the bishops of the Catholic Church.

37. Where did the Lord's Prayer (the Our Father) come from?

From the Lord Himself, in answer to His disciples' prayer: "Lord, teach us to pray" (Luke 11:1).

38. Where did the Ten Commandments come from?

From God, through His prophet Moses. They were reaffirmed by Christ, who said: "Do not think that I have come to abolish the law and the prophets; I have come not to abolish them but to fulfil them" (Matthew 5:17). Christ summarized them in the two great commandments to love God and neighbor (Matthew 22:35-40).

39. What, then, is the origin of the whole Catholic religion?

Christ. It all stems from and rests on Christ.

40. What is the form, or nature, or character, of the whole Catholic religion?

Christ. It all forms the identity of Christ in the Christian.

41. What is the end and the purpose of the whole Catholic religion?

Christ. Union with Christ is the whole end and purpose.

42. Will this religion give me peace?

Yes, because "religion" means "relationship" with God in Christ. No *thing* can give you peace, for the effect cannot be greater than the cause. Only a person can give a person peace.

43. Why must this person be God?

Because your heart was designed by God Himself, to be completely filled by Him alone.

You have made us for yourself, and [therefore] our hearts are restless until they rest in you. (St. Augustine)

In every heart there is a God-sized hole that the whole universe is not great enough to fill.

44. How can I find the God who can fill this hole in my heart?

You can't. That's the "bad news." But the "good news" is the Gospel that God has found you.

No one has ever seen God; the only-begotten Son, who is in the bosom of the Father, he has made him known. (John 1:18)

45. What must I do, then, to find the peace I seek?

Here is Jesus' answer:

"Come to me, all who labor and are heavy laden, and I will give you rest." (Matthew 11:28)

46. How can I come to Him if He lived two thousand years ago?

Because He still lives today. "He is not here; for he has risen" (Matthew 28:6). Unlike every other man, His tomb is empty. He promised His disciples, "I am with you always, to the close of the age" (Matthew 28:20).

47. Is He with us today only spiritually?

No. He touches us with His Body. His Church is His Body, and the Eucharist is His Body.

48. If I believe in Him and am baptized into His Body, what will happen to me?

- You will receive the very life of Christ: "I am the vine, you are the branches" (John 15:5).

- You will be filled with the Holy Spirit (Luke 3:16).

- Nothing will be able to separate you from God, in this world or in the next (Romans 8:31-39).

49. What is this new life called?

Scripture gives it many names, such
as salvation, sanctification, justifica-
tion, grace, regeneration, supernatu-
ral life, divine life, eternal life,
sharing the divine nature, the Kingdom of heaven, the Kingdom of
God, and being born again.

50. What must I do to receive this new life?

Christ's answer is that you must do three things:

- Repent of your sins (Matthew 4:17).

- Believe in Jesus Christ and be baptized "in the name of the Father and of the Son and of the Holy Spirit" (Matthew 28:19).

- Live in charity and forgiveness with your neighbor (Matthew 6:14).

51. What are sins?

Sin is any deliberate thought, word, deed, or omission that is contrary to God's will.

52. What is repentance?

Repentance is turning away from sin. It includes sorrow for sin, but it is not essentially a feeling, but an act of will. It is a choice *for* God and *against* sin.

53. Why must we repent?

Because in order to say yes to God, we must say no to sin, which is anti-God.

54. Doesn't the need for repentance make Christianity a gloomy religion?

Certainly not. Christianity is like a free life-saving operation for your soul. What is gloomy is to live in denial of the disease. Repentance makes us happy, not gloomy. For God, who is pure love, created us to share His own happiness and gave us His law as the true road to happiness. Therefore, we must turn from sin in order to enjoy happiness.

55. Must we be perfect?

No, but we must be *willing*, and we must make a sincere effort to obey God's will and avoid sin. God has provided the sacrament of reconciliation for us because He knows we are far from perfect.

56. Why is faith in Christ necessary?

Because only Christ can save us from sin and reunite us to God.

57. Why is baptism necessary?

Because Christ commanded it as the way of entering the Church.

58. Why is the Church necessary?

Because His Body is our salvation, and the Church is His Body.

59. Which Church is this?

There is only one. Christ does not have two bodies.

60. By what marks can it be known?

The "four marks of the Church" are these:

- one
- holy
- catholic (universal)
- apostolic

Christ said, "I am the way, and the truth, and the life; no one comes to the Father, but by me" (John 14:6). Christ is the only Savior, and the Church is His only Body.

Christ's Church extends far and wide, and she subsists in many places outside the visible Catholic Church. But its fullness subsists visibly only in the Church He Himself founded and authorized to teach in His name.

God is very gracious, "not wishing that any should perish, but that all should reach repentance" (2 Peter 3:9). And because God is so gracious, He has given us one way of salvation and marked it clearly.

Christ promised that all who seek find (Matthew 7:8). The Church teaches this:

Those also can attain to salvation who through no fault of their own do not know the Gospel of Christ or His Church, yet sincerely seek God and moved by grace strive by their deeds to do His will as it is known to them through the dictates of conscience. (Lumen Gentium, n. 16)

63. Why is the Church better than other religious organizations?

Because she is not a "religious organization." She is an extension of the Incarnation, the Body of the one Christ.

64. Is the Church human or divine?

Like Christ, she has a divine nature and a human nature. Unlike Christ, her human nature is far from perfect. Nevertheless, she is our concrete connection with Christ Himself, especially in the sacrament of the Eucharist.

65. Doesn't the Church keep us from God by multiplying intermediaries between us and God?

Exactly the opposite. The whole purpose of an intermediary is to *link*, not separate. Christ is the link between God and man, and His Church is the individual's link to Christ. As God made Himself concrete, visible, and available to us in Christ, so Christ made Himself concrete, visible, and available to us in His Church.

66. Does God work everywhere, even outside His Church?

God works everywhere.

67. So, what is the meaning of life?

God.